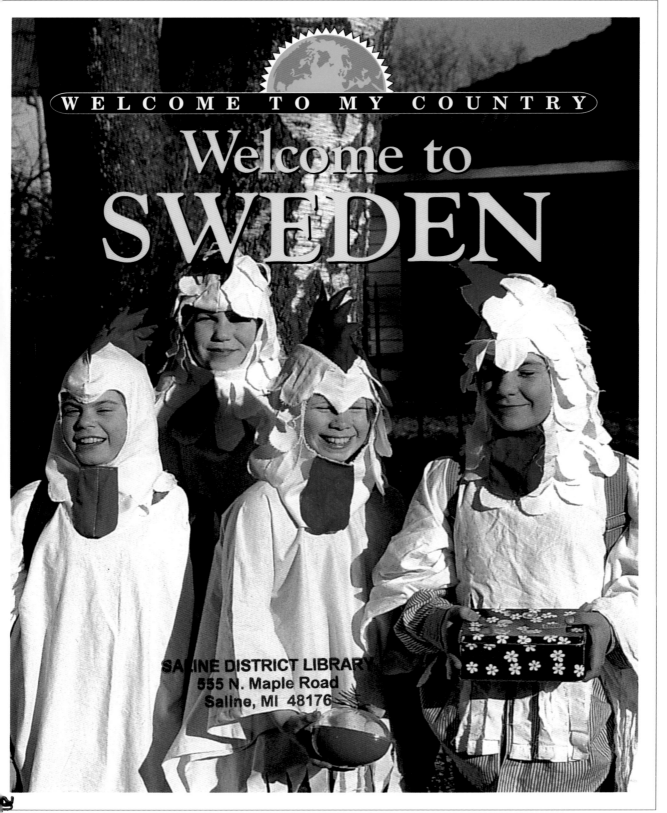

# WELCOME TO MY COUNTRY

# Welcome to
# SWEDEN

**Gareth Stevens Publishing**
A WORLD ALMANAC EDUCATION GROUP COMPANY

Written by
**VIMALA ALEXANDER/MICHELE WAGNER**

Edited in USA by
**DOROTHY L. GIBBS**

Designed by
**GEOSLYN LIM**

Picture research by
**SUSAN JANE MANUEL**

First published in North America in 2002 by
**Gareth Stevens Publishing**
A World Almanac Education Group Company
330 West Olive Street, Suite 100
Milwaukee, Wisconsin 53212 USA

Please visit our web site at:
www.garethstevens.com
For a free color catalog describing
Gareth Stevens Publishing's list of high-quality
books and multimedia programs,
call 1-800-542-2595 or
fax your request to (414) 332-3567.

© **TIMES MEDIA PRIVATE LIMITED 2002**
Originated and designed by
Times Editions
An imprint of Times Media Private Limited
A member of the Times Publishing Group
Times Centre, 1 New Industrial Road
Singapore 536196
http://www.timesone.com.sg/te

**Library of Congress Cataloging-in-Publication Data**
Alexander, Vimala.
Welcome to Sweden / Vimala Alexander and Michele Wagner.
p. cm. — (Welcome to my country)
Summary: An overview of the geography, history, government,
economy, people, and culture of Sweden.
ISBN 0-8368-2540-3 (lib. bdg.)
1. Sweden — Juvenile literature. [1. Sweden.] I. Wagner, Michele.
II. Title. III. Series.
DL609.A55   2002
948.5—dc21                  2002022384

Printed in Malaysia

1 2 3 4 5 6 7 8 9 06 05 04 03 02

**PICTURE CREDITS**
Art Directors and Trip Photo Library:
   3 (top), 5, 8, 26, 28 (both), 38, 41
Bes Stock: cover, 18
Jan Butchofsky-Houser: 40
Camera Press: 3 (bottom), 9, 31,
   36 (bottom)
Embassy of Sweden: 14, 15 (top),
   15 (center), 29 (both), 44 (both)
Focus Team – Italy: 7, 27
Hulton Getty/Archive Photos: 10, 11,
   12, 13, 15 (bottom)
Blaine Harrington III: 22, 23, 25, 45
Dave G. Houser: 2, 4, 6, 19, 30, 32,
   33, 37
The Hutchison Library: 21, 35
Björn Klingwall: 1, 20, 24
Bosse Lind: 3 (center)
Hakan Pettersson: 16 (top)
Photobank: 43
Roy Roberts: 17
Topham Picturepoint: 16 (bottom),
   34, 36 (top), 39

Digital Scanning by Superskill Graphics Pte Ltd

# Contents

Words that appear in the glossary are printed in **boldface** type the first time they occur in the text.

# Welcome to Sweden!

In Sweden, winter days are dark as night, and summer nights stay daytime bright. The land features highlands and lowlands, forests and plains. Its history ranges from Viking raids and civil wars to steady peace and **neutrality**. Let's visit this country of **contrasts** and find out more about its peaceful people.

**Opposite:** The style of the buildings in Stockholm's Gamla Stan, or Old Town, makes this area look like the Middle Ages.

**Below:** These Swedish children are dressed up in traditional clothing to perform in a folk dancing contest.

## The Flag of Sweden

The Swedish flag, officially adopted in 1906, has a gold Scandinavian Cross on a deep blue background. The cross symbolizes Sweden's Christian heritage. Blue and gold are colors in a Swedish coat of arms from 1364.

# The Land

With an area of 173,731 square miles (449,964 square kilometers), Sweden is the largest country in Scandinavia and the fourth largest country in Europe. It is surrounded by Norway, Finland, the Gulf of Bothnia, and the Baltic Sea, and it includes the islands of Gotland and Öland, off its southeastern coast. Denmark is just across a narrow **strait** from the country's southwestern coast.

**Below:** Spruce and pine forests cover areas of Sweden in the far north that are part of Lapland. Lapland includes northern areas of Norway, Finland, and Russia, too.

**Left:** Stockholm is in the Svealand region. Besides being Sweden's capital, Stockholm is the country's most important business center.

Norrland is the largest of Sweden's three main regions. Few people live in this mountainous northern area, which is partly in the Arctic Circle. Sweden's highest peak, Mount Kebnekaise, is in Norrland. Svealand, the central region, has both highlands and lowlands and contains the country's largest lakes, Vänern and Vättern. In the southern Götaland region, Skåne county is a heavily populated agricultural area.

## Climate

Sweden has mild weather even though it is so far north. Winds warmed by the **North Atlantic Current** keep summer temperatures at around 60° Fahrenheit (15° Celsius). In winter, temperatures fall as low as −40° F (−40° C) in the north but stay between 23° and 32° F (−5° and 0° C) in the south. North of the Arctic Circle, the Sun shines day and night from May to July. The winter months are in darkness day and night.

**Above:** Wildflowers brighten Sweden's countryside in spring. This field is in Uppsala.

## Plants and Animals

More than half of Sweden is covered with forests, mostly pine, fir, and birch in the north and elm, oak, maple, ash, and beech in the south. The treeless mountains have **alpine** plants such as dwarf birch and willows.

Bears and reindeer are common animals in northern Sweden. Moose, foxes, and hares are found throughout the country. Salmon and herring are two of Sweden's many kinds of fish.

**Below:**
The Sami people of Lapland raise herds of reindeer in the northern forests of Sweden.

# History

The first signs of human life in Sweden date back to 9000 B.C. Most of the early tribes were **nomads** or farmers. By the ninth century A.D., the Svear (Swedes) were the country's main inhabitants.

The Vikings were a powerful force in Sweden from the ninth century to the eleventh century. In the beginning, they were fierce pagan warriors, but in the tenth century, many Vikings became Christians. Vikings then helped spread Christianity throughout Sweden.

**Left:** Prehistoric cave paintings, called petroglyphs, can be seen at the Museum of Rock Carvings in Tanum. This petroglyph from the Bronze Age shows three human figures holding axes.

**Left:** Margaret I (1353–1412) was **regent** of Norway and Denmark when Swedish noblemen asked for her help to overthrow Albert of Mecklenburg. Although her great-nephew Erik was crowned king of the Kalmar Union in 1397, Margaret continued to rule until she died.

From 1248, the Folkung **dynasty** ruled in Sweden. In 1363, however, the Swedish nobility gave the throne to Albert of Mecklenburg. Albert was defeated in 1389 by Margaret I, who ruled Sweden, Norway, and Denmark as the Kalmar Union until her death in 1412. Erik of Pomerania took the throne after her, but only until 1439.

## After the Kalmar Union

Gustav I Vasa became the king of Sweden in 1523. Under his rule, the country broke away from the Kalmar Union and developed a centralized government and a strong army.

Monarchs after Gustav struggled through three centuries of warfare. In 1809, Denmark defeated Sweden in the Napoleonic Wars. In 1814, however, Sweden defeated Denmark and formed a union with Norway that lasted until 1905.

# Growth and Prosperity

Until the late 1800s, the economy of Sweden depended on agriculture. By the turn of the century, a growing population was moving to the cities to work in the country's new industries.

To protect its economic interests, Sweden stayed neutral through World War I (1914–1918). After the war, the demand for Swedish goods increased sharply, but this prosperity ended with the **Great Depression** of the 1930s.

**Below:** King Oscar II opened the Swedish **parliament** in 1905. Swedish men were given the right to vote in 1907. By 1921, all Swedish citizens could vote.

## Neutrality and Stability

Sweden was neutral again through World War II (1939–1945) and is still neutral today. New economic growth continued until the mid-1970s, when worldwide economic problems brought rising prices and high unemployment. Today, Sweden is a member of both the United Nations and the European Union, a large economic organization.

**Left:** Carl XVI Gustaf has been Sweden's king and its official representative since 1973. Queen Silvia is his **consort**.

## Queen Kristina (1626–1689)

Crowned queen of Sweden at age eighteen, Kristina was known for her wisdom and for supporting the arts. She encouraged trade and kept class rivalries in the country from developing into **civil war**.

Queen Kristina

## Fredrika Bremer (1801–1865)

Born in Swedish Finland, Fredrika Bremer wrote popular novels that stood up for women's rights. Her 1856 book, *Hertha*, helped bring about both political and economic reforms for Swedish women.

Fredrika Bremer

## Raoul Wallenberg (1912–1947?)

In 1944, Raoul Wallenberg, who was from a wealthy Swedish family, saved thousands of Hungarian Jews from death in Nazi **concentration camps**. He disappeared later that year. Some reports say he died in a Russian prison in 1947.

Raoul Wallenberg

# Government and the Economy

In Sweden's constitutional monarchy, the king is the chief of state, but all government decisions are made by the prime minister and an appointed cabinet. The *Riksdag* (RICKS-dahg), which is Sweden's parliament, elects the prime minister and passes all laws. The laws are upheld by district courts, courts of appeal, and a supreme court.

**Above:** Göran Persson was first elected Sweden's prime minister in 1996, and he was reelected in 1998.

**Left:** Sweden's parliament meets in the Riksdag building, which is the center of political activity in Stockholm, the country's capital.

**Left:** The police force in Sweden has both male and female officers. These two officers are on patrol in the city of Stockholm.

## Local Governments

Sweden is divided into 21 counties and 284 **municipalities**. The counties are run by governors and county boards appointed by the national government. Municipalities are governed by elected assemblies. Ombudsmen appointed by the Riksdag investigate complaints against the government at all levels.

**Left:** Almost half of the cars made in Sweden are sold to the United States. The most popular Swedish cars are Volvo and SAAB.

# The Economy

Sweden has a strong, steady economy, and its annual production of goods and services is one of the highest in the world. Among the country's main manufacturing industries are metals, engineering, and electronics.

Many Swedish workers, especially women, have jobs in service industries, such as business, education, and health care. Few Swedes work in agriculture today, yet the nation's farms produce some of the world's highest yields.

## Natural Resources

Its forests are one of Sweden's most important natural resources. Wood and paper products are among the country's major exports. Sweden also has rich mineral deposits, including gold, iron, and copper, but it lacks **fossil fuels**. Almost half of the nation's imports are oil and petroleum products.

## Transportation

Well-built roads and efficient public bus systems make travel in Sweden easy. Sweden also has three major airports and twenty shipping ports.

**Above:** Ferries are becoming a popular way to travel between Sweden and its neighboring countries.

# People and Lifestyle

Almost all Swedish people speak the same language, belong to the same religion, and have German ancestors. Swedes enjoy a high standard of living. Most live in the cities, but many also have homes in the countryside, where they spend their vacations. Southern Sweden, especially in Skåne county and the central and coastal lowlands, is the most heavily populated.

**Below:** Because of their common German heritage, most Swedes have blond hair, blue eyes, and fair skin.

People from Greece, Turkey, and Chile, as well as **immigrants** from other Scandinavian countries, live in Sweden. Finnish people first arrived in the 1500s, but most came in the late 1960s. About 500,000 Finns live in Sweden today. Among the country's earliest settlers were the Sami, known also as Lapps. About 20,000 Sami live in Sweden. Some are reindeer herders.

**Above:** Outdoor marketplaces in Stockholm and many other towns and villages are well-stocked with fresh fruits and vegetables.

## Family Life

Although families are very important in Swedish society, most of them are small. Sweden's cities do not have enough space to provide housing for large families. Children, nevertheless, are highly valued. Swedish parents receive money from the government for each child, and high-quality day care is provided for children whose mothers have jobs. Swedish law even allows parents to take time off from their jobs to care for their children.

**Above:** Low-cost government loans are available to Swedish parents so they can buy homes in which to raise their children.

Older people are valued and well-cared for in Sweden, too, by younger family members as well as by the government. Benefits for the elderly include low-cost housing and a public health care system.

**Welfare** benefits contribute greatly to Sweden's high standard of living and have made working outside the home possible for more Swedish women.

**Left:** Many elderly people in Sweden live by themselves, but younger family members visit them frequently.

# Education

Sweden's well-organized, high-quality education system is free to everyone. Children start elementary school, called *grundskola* (GRUND-school-ah), at the age of seven, but many children attend preschool at age six.

Every child must attend nine years of elementary school. During the first six years, all students study the same subjects. From the seventh year on,

**Left:**
About 2 percent of Swedish students attend elementary school at a private, rather than public, institution. Private schools are open to all students and are approved by Sweden's national education agency.

students choose their own subjects.
All students must study English for
four years, starting in the third year
of elementary school.

High school, or *gymnasieskola*
(jim-NAH-zee-eh-school-ah), is not
required, but nearly 90 percent of
Swedish students attend. High school
lasts three years and prepares students
either for jobs or for more education at
one of Sweden's thirteen universities.

**Above:** Some high school students in Sweden still follow the Scandinavian tradition of wearing a white hat during their graduation ceremony.

**Left:** Although most Swedes are not churchgoers, they still consider the Lutheran faith an important part of their lives and their traditions.

# Religion

About 90 percent of Swedish people belong to the Evangelical Lutheran Church of Sweden, but most Swedish Lutherans go to church only on major holy days and for religious events, such as baptisms and weddings.

Very small numbers of Swedes are Catholics, Muslims, Buddhists, Hindus, Jews, or non-Lutheran Protestants.

## Folk Beliefs

Before Christianity came to Sweden, the Vikings had their own beliefs, which included **Norse** gods, such as Thor, god of thunder, and Odin, god of wisdom and war. The Vikings also believed in giants, dwarfs, and elves.

The Sami had folk beliefs, too, and they had village **shamans**, who gave them advice from the gods. The Sami believe that every object has a soul and there is a god in every force of nature.

**Below:** Very high, arched ceilings are an architectural feature inside many Swedish churches.

# Language

The Swedish language is very similar to the languages of Norway, Denmark, and Iceland. All of these Scandinavian languages have German roots. A few Swedish words come from the English and French languages.

Modern Swedish started in 1526, with a translation of the Bible's New Testament, and was modeled after the Swedish spoken in the Stockholm area. Spoken Swedish has a singsong sound.

**Above:** Many of the houses in Sweden have a handpainted mailbox with the family's name on it.

**Below:** This sign is written in modern Swedish.

# Literature

Literature in Sweden dates back to the 1200s, and the translation of the Bible into Swedish, in the 1500s, was one of the most important literary events.

Twentieth-century writer August Strindberg (1849–1912) is considered Sweden's greatest author. His stories, plays, and poems made bold statements about society. Selma Lagerlöf was the first woman and the first Swede to win the Nobel Prize for Literature. Astrid Lindgren's books have been translated into more than seventy languages.

# Arts

Swedish artists, architects, musicians, and filmmakers are known around the world. Anders Zorn (1860–1920) is famous for his paintings of Swedish village life. Carl Larsson (1853–1919) is widely known for the watercolor portraits of his home and family. The monuments and fountains created by Carl Milles (1875–1955) made him Sweden's best-known sculptor in the early 1900s.

**Above:**
This monument in Stockholm, called *Europa and the Bull*, is one of Carl Milles's famous sculptures.

# Architecture

For centuries, Swedish buildings have been designed to blend in with their surroundings. Today's architecture features simple, practical designs that let in as much natural light as possible.

# Music

Swedes love music, from traditional folk music to symphonies to jazz and pop. Nineteenth-century composer Franz Berwald (1796–1868) had an enormous impact on the development of the Swedish symphony. ABBA is a world-famous Swedish pop group.

**Left:** Swedish businessman Ingvar Kamprad (1926– ) started IKEA in 1943. This international furniture company specializes in practical items for the home that reflect modern Swedish design.

## Performing Arts

Sweden actively supports a wide range of performing arts, including theater, opera, and dance. Stockholm's Royal Dramatic Theater, founded in 1788, has many foreign plays among its annual productions. Opera houses stage both classical and modern performances. Folk dancing and international dances, such as the flamenco, are now almost as popular in Sweden as ballet.

Directors Ingmar Bergman and Lasse Hallström and movie stars Greta Garbo and Ingrid Bergman have made some Swedish films international hits.

# Handicrafts

The Swedes have made high-quality, handcrafted products since the early 1800s. Many of them are woodcrafts. Brightly painted wooden horses known as *Dalahäst*, or Dala horses, are famous Swedish carvings. Glassmaking in Sweden dates back to 2000 B.C. Today, the Kingdom of Crystal in the Småland Highlands is the glassworks center of the country. Other Swedish handicrafts include ceramics, silver, and textiles.

**Below:**
Dala horses are made in the county of Dalarna. This worker is sanding some Dala horses so that they can be painted.

# Leisure

Outdoor activities are very popular in Sweden. Favorite pastimes include walking, hunting, and fishing. The Kungsleden, or Royal Route, is a well-known hiking trail in northern Sweden. It is 300 miles (483 kilometers) long! Fishing is so popular that Swedes cut holes in the ice on frozen lakes and rivers to fish in winter.

**Below:** Swedes enjoy cycling and picnicking in the country's many parks. They also like to get away from the cities as often as possible.

Enjoying nature is extremely important to Swedes. The Swedish government has even passed a law known as *Allemansrätten* (AH-leh-manz-reh-ten), or the Right of Public Access, which allows anyone to walk, camp, or even pick flowers or berries in any field or forest in the country.

Besides outdoor activities, Swedes enjoy going to theaters, museums, and art galleries. They also like to read, play chess, and visit with friends.

**Above:**
This Swedish family is out for a ride in a horsecart. Many Swedes spend weekends and vacations in the countryside.

# Sports

Its different landscapes and climates make Sweden a perfect place for both winter and summer sports. Skiing, ice hockey, and bandy are popular winter sports. Bandy is played like ice hockey, but with a ball instead of a puck.

**Above:** Skiing is, by far, the most popular winter sport in Sweden. Thousands of Swedes compete each year in the country's many skiing events.

**Left:** In 1990, Sweden's Stefan Edberg was the number one tennis player in the world. He beat Germany's Boris Becker in the Wimbledon Championships that year.

Soccer and tennis are Sweden's favorite summer sports. In 1994, the Swedish national soccer team placed third in the World Cup Championships. Swedish tennis players Mats Wilander, Stefan Edberg, and Björn Bjorg are known throughout the world.

**Below:** Large numbers of men and women compete in the annual Stockholm Marathon, which is held in June.

A type of cross-country running called orienteering is quickly gaining popularity in Sweden and now attracts about 100,000 runners. Table tennis, badminton, and golf are also popular. Sweden has over 360 golf courses.

# Festivals

Every year on April 30, the people of Sweden celebrate the arrival of spring with singing and bonfires. This festival, which began in Viking times, is called *Valborgsmassoafton*, or Walpurgis Night. Easter is a religious celebration in spring. On Easter Sunday, families go to church, then have a big meal together at home. Boys and girls dress up as Easter witches and visit their neighbors, who give them small gifts.

**Below:** Families and friends gather to eat herring and fresh potatoes on Midsummer's Eve. This celebration began as a harvest festival. Today, it is a national holiday, held on the Friday closest to June 24.

December 13 is Saint Lucia Day. A girl dressed in white and wearing a crown of candles leads a group of children on visits to hospitals and schools. The children sing and pass out *Lussekatter* (LOOSE-cah-ter), which are sweet, **saffron** buns.

Christmas is the most important religious festival in Sweden. People decorate their homes and bake special treats. On Christmas Day, they attend *julottan* (YULE-ooh-tan), an early morning church service.

**Above:** Santa Claus visits some Sami children in Swedish Lapland. Children all over Sweden look forward to a personal visit and special gifts from Santa Claus on Christmas Eve.

# Food

**Above:** Sweden has many elegant restaurants. This dining room, which is in the Veranden restaurant, has a good view of Stockholm.

Swedish food is usually simple, with lots of fish and potato dishes. Salmon is a favorite fish. Swedes prepare it smoked, **marinated**, or preserved with dill and salt. They like *lutfisk* (LOOT-fisk), too. It is cod soaked in **lye**. Served as a traditional Christmas dish, lutfisk is fried lightly in butter and is seasoned with salt and pepper.

A smörgåsbord (SMORE-gose-bord) is a Swedish buffet that serves a wide variety of foods, from pickled herring and other appetizers to smoked reindeer and *köttbullar* (shot-BULL-ar), or meatballs. *Ostkaka* (oost-KAK-ah), a popular Swedish dessert, is a cheesecake that is topped with fresh fruit or jam.

**Left:** Late July to early September is crayfish season in Sweden. The crayfish are boiled with dill, sugar, and salt and are eaten by hand.

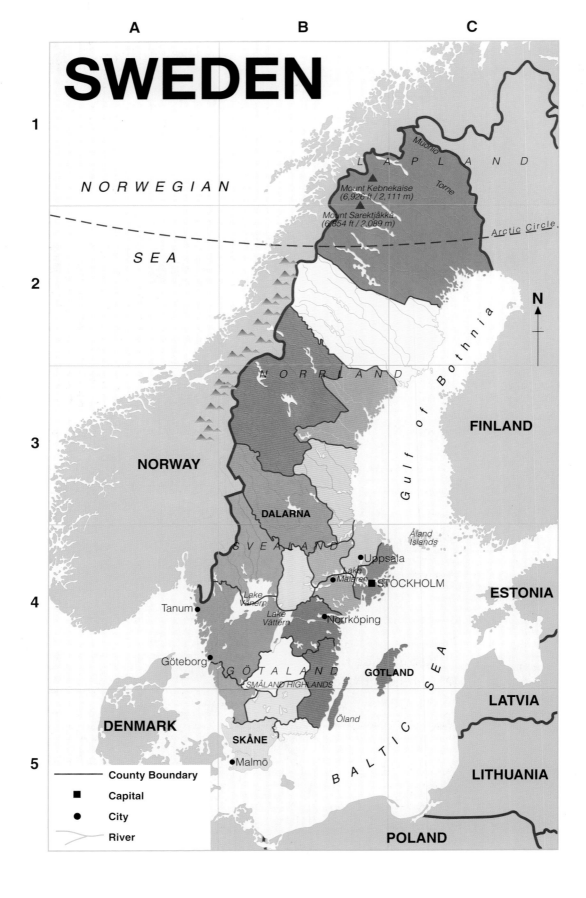

# SWEDEN

**Above:** A fisherman repairs his boat at his home on the western coast of Sweden.

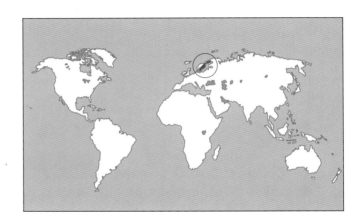

# Quick Facts

| | |
|---|---|
| **Official Name** | Kingdom of Sweden |
| **Capital** | Stockholm |
| **Official Language** | Swedish |
| **Population** | 8,875,053 (July 2001 estimate) |
| **Land Area** | 173,731 square miles (449,964 square km) |
| **Highest Point** | Mount Kebnekaise 6,926 feet (2,111 m) |
| **Major Rivers** | Muonio, Torne |
| **Major Lakes** | Lake Mälaren, Lake Vänern, Lake Vättern |
| **Major Cities** | Göteborg, Malmö, Norrköping, Stockholm, Uppsala |
| **Main Religion** | Lutheran |
| **Major Festivals** | Easter (March/April) |
| | Walpurgis Night (April 30) |
| | Midsummer's Day (June) |
| | Saint Lucia Day (December 13) |
| | Christmas Day (December 25) |
| **Currency** | Krona (SEK 10.71 = U.S. $1 as of 2002) |

**Opposite:** Musicians perform on the streets of Gamla Stan, or Old Town, in Stockholm.

# Glossary

**alpine:** belonging to the Alps or other mountainous areas that are above the tree line.

**civil war:** a war between sections of the same country or different groups of citizens within that country.

**concentration camps:** fenced, guarded areas where people are held prisoner, usually for political reasons.

**consort:** the wife or husband of a ruler.

**contrasts:** differences between things that can be compared.

**dynasty:** a family of rulers who inherit their power.

**fossil fuels:** fuels, such as coal and natural gas, that are formed by the remains of dead plants and animals.

**Great Depression:** the worldwide economic failure that followed the U.S. stock market crash of 1929.

**immigrants:** people who move from their home countries to live permanently in other countries.

**lye:** a harsh substance used to make strong cleaning products.

**marinated:** soaked in a seasoned liquid, before cooking, to add flavor.

**municipalities:** cities or towns that have their own local governments.

**neutrality:** a position of not taking part or helping either side in a dispute such as a war.

**nomads:** people who have no permanent home and move as a group from place to place.

**Norse:** having to do with Norway or ancient Scandinavia.

**North Atlantic Current:** the currents of the Atlantic Ocean that bring warm, Gulf Stream waters far north.

**parliament:** a group of government representatives who are elected by the people to make the nation's laws.

**regent:** a person who rules a country for a period of time when the king or queen is not able to rule.

**saffron:** a product that comes from the flower of a crocus plant and is used to color foods orange-yellow.

**shamans:** priestlike people who use magic to cure illnesses and to control certain events.

**strait:** a narrow body of water that passes between two land masses and connects two larger bodies of water.

**welfare:** having to do with social services for citizens, such as health care and housing, that are paid for by the government.

# More Books to Read

*Annika's Secret Wish.* Beverly Lewis (Bethany House)

*Christmas in Sweden.* Cheryl L. Enderlein (Bridgestone Books)

*Do You Know Pippi Longstocking?* Astrid Lindgren (R & S Books)

*The Grandchildren of the Vikings.* Matti A. Pitkanen and Reijo Harkonen (Carolrhoda Books)

*Per and the Dala Horse.* Rebecca Hickox (Bantam Books)

*Sweden. The Countries* series. Kate A. Furlong (Abdo & Daughters)

*Sweden. Festivals of the World* series. Monica Rabe (Gareth Stevens)

*Sweden in Pictures. Visual Geography* series. Jo McDonald (Lerner)

*Viking Life. Early Civilizations* series. J. A. Guy (Barrons Juveniles)

*The Wonderful Adventures of Nils.* Selma Lagerlöf (Dover)

# Videos

*Christmas in Sweden.* (Spoken Arts)

*Families of Sweden.* (Master Communication)

*Scandinavia: Denmark, Sweden and Norway.* (Questar)

*Super Cities: Stockholm.* (Library Video)

# Web Sites

www.royalcourt.se/net/Royal+Court

www.stockholmtown.com

www.sverigeturism.se/smorgasbord

www.visit-sweden.com

Due to the dynamic nature of the Internet, some web sites stay current longer than others. To find additional web sites, use a reliable search engine with one or more of the following keywords to help you locate information on Sweden. Keywords: *Dala horse, Kingdom of Crystal, Lapland, smörgåsbord, Stockholm, Vikings.*

# Index